LEAP OF LIFE

BOOK OF VERSE

BIKRAMJIT SEN

To the quiet whispers of inspiration that dance in the spaces between heartbreaks,

For the untamed emotions that weave the tapestry of the soul,

This collection of poetry is dedicated.

To the moonlit nights that cradle dreams,

And the sun-kissed mornings that breathe life into verses,

To the rhythm of life that echoes in every line,

This book is dedicated to you.

To the ones who find solace in the symphony of words,

Who seek refuge in the sanctuary of metaphor and rhyme,

For the kindred spirits who understand the language of the heart

This book is a tribute to our shared journey

To the late-night musings and dawn reflections,

For the moments of joy and shadows of sorrow,

This book is a tribute to the kaleidoscope of emotions we share

To the family whose unwavering support is my anchor

And who lent their ears to my soul's melodies

Your presence is woven into the fabric of these pages

To the readers who embark on this intimate literary journey,

May these words find home in the chambers of your hearts,

For it is to you, the silent companions of my literary odyssey,

That this book is wholly dedicated

With gratitude and love,

Bikramjit Sen

Contents

Contents

ॐ गं गणपतये नमः

Preface

Welcome to a collection of poems that serves as a compass through the landscapes of inspiration, motivation, spirituality, and raw emotion. In these verses, find encouragement to navigate the challenges, motivation to reach new heights, and a spiritual resonance that transcends the ordinary.

Discover the strength within you through motivational poems, rise above adversity, and tap into your untapped potential. Journey into the spiritual realms, where these verses echo the universal quest for meaning, purpose, and connection.

Embrace the authenticity of emotional expression, where vulnerability becomes a source of strength. Each poem is a brushstroke, contributing to the canvas of our shared human experience.

May these verses be companions on your journey, resonating with the melody of your heart and soul. Welcome to the poetic odyssey of inspiration, motivation, spirituality, and emotion.

Acknowledgements

In the alchemy of crafting this collection of verses, I am deeply grateful to those whose influence and support have shaped these poems into existence. With sincere appreciation, I extend my thanks to:

My Muse- for the whimsical dances in the moonlit corridors of imagination, inspiring the language of emotions to flow from pen to paper.

Family and friends- whose enduring love and encouragement form the bedrock of my creative spirit. Your belief in my journey fuels the fire within.

Mentors and teachers- whose guidance and insights have been the compass steering my poetic ship through uncharted waters. Your wisdom is etched into every stanza.

Readers- the silent companions who breathe life into these verses, finding resonance in the cadence of shared experiences. Your interpretation adds depth and meaning to these lines.

Editors and Publishers- for their invaluable contributions in refining and bringing these words to the world. Your dedication to the craft is truly appreciated.

The Natural World- for providing a canvas of beauty and complexity, offering endless inspiration in every sunrise, sunset, storm, and quiet moment of reflection.

The Quiet Corners and Society-where solitude met the inspiration, and the symphony of life provided a backdrop to the creation of these verses.

To every soul who contributed in ways seen or unseen, your influence is embedded in the lines and spaces of this collection. Thank you for being part of this poetic tradition.

With profound gratitude,

Bikramjit Sen

Poet Bio

Born in Kolkata, India, on December 13, 1996, Bikramjit Sen is a prolific author and poet with a profound passion for storytelling. He has co-authored numerous anthologies and stands as the author of eight distinctive books, showcasing his versatility in both prose and poetry.

His literary journey includes notable works such as "Twenty Three: Collection of Short Stories," "Ashwatdhama: Menace," "Ecstasy: A Poetry Collection and Leap of Life: Book of Verse along with Svairakalpana, all published by NotionPress Publishing. Additionally, Bikramjit has crafted meaningful narratives with Potentially Divine Souls, Bouquet: A Collection of Poems and Pearls: Poetic Pieces, each published by Evincepub Publishing.

Bikramjit's literary prowess has garnered recognition and accolades, marking him as one of the 100 Inspiring Authors of India in 2018 by Indian Awaz...

His dedication to literature and the arts has also been celebrated with the prestigious Swami Vivekananda Excellence Award in 2019, presented by the Seva Youth Guild, both accolades bestowed upon him in the culturally rich City of Joy- Kolkata, India.

In each written piece, Bikramjit Sen weaves tales that resonate with readers, reflecting his deep understanding of the human experience and a commitment to inspire and engage through the power of words.

Bikramjit Sen

1. Farther future...

You don't know what the future has in store for you
You don't realise
That it holds nothing,
No Thing...
For you
It's simply nothing that the future holds that you think, it keeps holding
...awaiting you, except that inevitable hour...
When every pain ends in
substitutes...
When the heavens will shower 'flowers'
And what you considered yours will be taken to the pyre...
You will come to know,
You never were yours...
Your future holds nothing
Your future does not recognise you
My bad, your future does not know you
Neither does it have any presents
to present to you and thus impress you...
Nor does it carry the magic potion to undo things already done by you...
Yes, it's empty!
A vacuum...
Absolutely blank!
It's empty, it's blank!

Your present decides
The fate of your future
Your future holds nothing special
but you in your reports...
Whether you work for it, or not...
That is up to you...
But still, you will see
A FUTURE...
There is a future
A bright one or a light one
That's up to you
Whatever you make of it
In your perception, in your action
That's how it belongs to you...
How beautiful you make it,
it's completely up to you...
Or else it will arrive
With a lot of ugly, unanswered questions,
empty dashes, unusually blank spaces and whatnot...
Ellipsis, you see, no end-to-end narrative...
Staring at you with questionable eyes...
Creating ambiguity and ambivalence in your mind, the reader!
Yes, you read it right, you're the reader, you only, the writer of your
life...
You're both
In line with the double-edged sword!
Write what, you wish to read...
Or else be ready to stare at blank pages
That still needs to be filled with ink...

Read, read, and re-read...
Perhaps there is so much more...
To fill the store...
Grains need to be poured
A character waits in search of its author...
...every future awaits alike the inevitable hour...
As there is no present in future
The future holds nothing great!
Neither does it know you nor your present
It's you, completely you, completely
up to you, totally your presence
that makes a life great, a future truly possible...
Further is always present in your present
That has the potential to give you presents
As farther future...
Furthermore, further is no farther, farther is still near, near you...
You're your experimental story,
Life has given YOU!

2. Look around there, things inspiring...

Look around there...
Things Inspiring!
Look around,
there are things, inspiring!
What if, you're star-struck...
Isn't it so obvious to be so?
So many stars shining out
In this endless universe of possibilities...
Some came across hardships
Some created them
While crossing...
They started uprooting
Many so-thought dead...
Let it remain...
Let it remain there
Who knows what sprouts
From where...
Perhaps you didn't know
No end is permanent
From every end
There is the rise of the new...
I know one thing, I know nothing
In front of you, I don't stand a chance
At anything...

Nothing can take you to nothing
When nothing becomes everything...
Nothing can make you do nothing
Why are you always into something
Ever wondered why is there such a thing?
I wish I could have explained my thing
But as they say, time isn't ripe yet
To understand your everything in nothing
Nothing existed before nothing
Nothing will exist after nothing
Nothing is beyond nothing
Everything lies in being nothing
Things partying
Parting with things
Have learnt a great deal
To be close to nothing
Unlearning
After a great deal of learning
Get Up
Updo get
The thing
Called noTHING!

3. Tribute to my fire within...

Fire eats-up everything
That you put in...
This world of sorrows...
Ah! Everything is burning...
And in no-time
You are left with nothing!
Like fly ash, moments are fleeting...
They never settle down in the time zone
You're existing!
That alone makes you realise
Rest, take a deep breath...
Pause, and breathe!
What for are you running?
The futility of human endeavours
Is it ok to pause?
Yes, it is...
Existence doesn't mean running...
The tortoise too exists
Is it always moving?
In this movable world...
You become the icon of immovability!
That feeling of nothingness
While existing...
Is everything, you could ask for
If at all, you need to ask for anything...

Nothing is everything
Nothing means everything
That feeling of nothingness…
This means there's evenness in your personality
Signs of progress, growth within...
After toiling for lives
To look after your worldly duties
In each birth
You forgot the fire within
That kept silent and constantly kept burning...
The continuous blows of the worldly fire
Makes you other-worldly
Sooner or later
You toil to thank the inner fire
Burning within!
It makes it easier for you
To put a burning match to your worldliness
For the sake of the ONE otherworldly
You are not lonely from within
A fire is there, inside you, constantly burning...
And you are unaware...
No matter how far
That fire takes you in all activities of your life
It's helping you to progress spiritually!
That God-send light
Makes you understand the difference
Between the real and the imagined
Makes you free from
All the frivolities

And puts you in another zone
To put an end to your existential crisis
The fire within
Burns your inside first
And then what remains outside
For burning
You claim you've
Everything under control!
I ask, really?
Like fly-ash
Moments are fleeting
Never do they settle down
In the time zone, you're in...
Existing??
Crying?
Really!

4. Wait and watch...

I will rise from my flames like the phoenix
And make the world witness again
What I'm made of...
I'm a maverick
Born to make a place of my own...
I shall stand tall against all odds
That clouded my self-belief
And there will be a grand face-off!
A lot of things seem
Beyond my control
Right now
A few things are in me
In due time
That can make me steel
I shall be a man of steel
When I learn to let go most, without despair
And focus on the few that I've with me...
Making them my strong zone,
So strong that even things beyond control
Are influenced by the power of my control
On the things that I've in me...
This journey is a help indeed
To kill that acquired vanity
Sprouting in me...
I'll thrive...

Where the power of concentration lies
I merge my 'I'
Beyond is nothing
When within is everything...
All false limitations that I used to think
Are not my weaknesses
Like that, I wasn't meant to be...
Like that, I'm not
Like this, I'm
Things are in my stride
Now believing in me!
Everything is even-steven after death
It's a halt to all the madness growing inside
And outside of me...

5. Walk the Talk...

A lot has been talked about...
But who dares to walk the talk?
Are you one of them...
Who said a lot but failed to replicate
In action what you thought…
When it comes to you
You're a hypocrite...
Self-deception
How strange!
I mean look at yourself
In words always, in deeds never ever!
Even for once, my dear friend,
you never tried for yourself what you recommended...
Why?
How strange this can be?
When time's demand is to be strong
I dare you
Prove me wrong
Walk the talk
Leave all ambivalence
You know, not being ready
Won't do it for long...
No, it's never too late to make a start!
You just need to take that first step
Although it may sound like Herculean a task

Right now, may even give you the eerie feel of hell
But trust me, your trust in the process
Will sail you through all the ups and downs
That you're now truly ready to witness...
Most painful, huh, but certainly rewarding...
Courageous man!
COURAGE,
Where is your courage?
Courageous man: -
Invoke, what's lost to dread!
Be BRAVE and leave the rest...
You stooped to attain greatness
You became inert losing way
Oh c'mon, don't control...
Let your ADRENALINE gush forth
Strong, forever strong...

6. Run...

The world is on the run...
Hoarding and hoarding...
Not only now, but since ages
The worldly of the world
Have been doing so...
You've been rather slow!
Why share the disgrace
of becoming the first one to go?
You've thought,
It's better to accept
What comes of its own accord
And try not to try to hold to
Things that wish to explore
life after leaving you
at the first 'go...'
You've been too naive
To believe that
According to the world
You're a fool to let go
And not even try to bring in
Unlike the world-lie...
what never was yours!

7. At play...

The cats and dogs were at play
In the meanwhile, I rose above hatred
Finding the ONE God
sitting in the hearts of all,
I decided to rejoice at whatever I got...
You exist
You do exist
For me
Victorious or vanquished
Whatever be thy Will...
For me
I'll partake in the celebration of it...
Rest, I leave...
Where is my free will?
If you've scripted someone's win
Who can change it?
Perhaps, I'll embrace it
As MY WIN
With a soft smile shining on my lips
Because it's always you
Who is winning...
Isn't it sufficient to know...
Yes-yes, the triumph is of God
It's always U who is winning...
You've become uncountable existences

You've chosen to win through somebody else

Today, not me...

Better luck next time

For I won't give up on winning!

Hey, society,

What are you saying?

I'm all ears

Tell me...

Shall I give up on hope for that one reason that I did not win on some

occasions in my life?

No, never,

For I know today God is playing through them

No one knows tomorrow or for that case overmorrow

Against whom I'll be utilized

By the almighty to win...

Probably that day too shall soon come

When God will be mine

In the form of my victory

And not learnings...

Teachings, pages after pages

I've seen

History repeats itself

The Sun will again be shining

Till that time

Let me enjoy the lunar phase

Of my life

I'm more than happy to be the moon

Right now...

Radiating peace...

Cold, huh?
The warmth of my behaviour?
Tired of the scorching heat!

8. Brain-dead

The dead weight

that you carry over your shoulders

Yes, it's actually dead...

Brain!

You're brain-dead!

You don't see the difference between

the real and the unreal...

You are like the day-tides

One after the other

Society feeds you with lucrative jibes

And you don't reason, you don't argue with yourself to understand

What to go for and

how not to waste the remaining time...

You don't discriminate between your good and what unhealthy stuffs

are made of...

You see all things outside!

Never do you think that it's inside...

All is inside...

Everything is inside...

The brain that has been conditioned by society

To see according to its dictates

Can never approach the fight of life

With the same intensity

That you will, leaving your brain aside!

All the dead weight that you have been carrying as your burden

Needs an update, and a lease of new life
Release all toxins that were given to you
As doses of fabricated knowledge
And inhale the freshness surrounding every moment of your existence!
Worldly opium intake makes your brain sleep in no time...
The sleep persists till you deliberately
Try to wake up from the effect
Of the poison of position that has turned everything
upside-down in this spiritual fight!
The jinx needs to be broken
Or else you won't have peace
Even for a moment!
Why are you looking for shoulders to cry on?
See, aren't your shoulders broad enough...
To accommodate you, the real you, keeping your brain aside!

9. Big Unfinished...

Big statues of God
Have surrounded me
From all sides
I'm unable to move
Except towards paradise
On the count of four
Determine the things you wish to do
And the things you won't even if told
Thank you, God, for this beautiful human body; for making me realise
you
In life...
Everything is scattered in directions galore...
You think, whether the things you pick...
Were ever truly yours...
That power that makes you commit suicide
Will not lead you to glory
Whatever you do or say
Remember, Ramakrishna, the name, is the way...
Life is a foggy weather
Not only this winter season
Life clears up as we progress...
And everything that we leave behind
Regains their true haze...
Don't you worry child…
The stars are shining brighter for you

The stats are in your favour
No one is against you...
Who will you rescue and from whom?
Your own shadow betrays you...
Sorry to say this as your misfortune
Perhaps you are not born for this alone...
One and all must go the other shore!

10. Hello Morn...

Why so morose
in this motley universe?
This is a place of mirth...
What are you worrying about?
Are you morbid?
Yes!
Good, you are real...
Don't abort!
Don't stop...
Let your soul sleep
May your body, work
Let your body rest
May your soul, work
Whichever the way
One has to work, for another...
That is the way, that has been the way...
For how long, I don't know much...
Why this clash of active and passive...
Whatever you're, you belong to others, not yours;
you never were...
You are your help
as well as that of others
In this vast universe
A blessing to mankind in disguise
What for is this chaos?

Alas! SILENCE WAS REAL...

• 22 •

11. Transition

Your road to endless possibilities
Opens-up here...
The transition always
Brings something new,
positive and sublime with itself
This fresh transitional phase;
Shall be an ecstatic blessing
Not a disgrace
Elements of the past
Elements from the present
Parenting you equally in your existence
The preceding age
The forthcoming one
Somewhere in between the twin-you...
You live in this moment!
The bygone moments,
your cherished ideals...
Another year of life fading away...
But see, you haven't perished...
As of yet, I can say
Hope for the best
Prepare for the worst
Continue the way you've been doing
Try, burn, fight it out
Everyday

Endure, persevere, forbear
You have been doing good
Through all thick and thin
Please see the light coming your way
Now, no more away...
Far, far is ignorance
Near, near is strength!
Oblivious to parallel existences
You keep humming...
Old is finishing in new
Time has evolved
Dualities have ceased to exist
Now, we aren't anymore two!

12. Foggy Clutter

Amidst the fog
You see one light
Not far away
From you
Within the reach of your eyes
You ponder about this one light
When nature has wrapped everything in white, how dare it show its
original side...
The true face of emancipation,
experiencing the blessed joy of liberty...
How dare it be, as it is;
being carefree!
What does it take to be like this?
At what price is this liberty?
According to the current of the times,
when nature wants to change it,
embody as something different,
with someone else's qualities...
Emaciated society,
unnerving and harrowing times,
events of failure all around...
This light is a sport, amidst all this...
It smiles...
From where does it muster the much-needed courage and power to
strike?

Against the blowing wind...
It blows its own tune,
I'm fine, I'm good, I'm okay...
Everything is at their respective places...
With all due regard to each and all
From the standpoint of the theory of relativity
Nothing can be classified as "this only";
that isn't liberty!
Endearing change;
are you in this, with me?
Or shall I walk alone
as I have been doing thus far
on that path, where there is truth, joy, and beauty...

13. Unfinished

When nothing seems fair
When nothing seems right
When all the darkness engulfs you from all sides
You find your essence lost somewhere in the sands of time
Dreary, deserted, left to wail for the rest of your life...
Too far away
Still far near
Paradox it is...
Dark clouds are slowly scattering away...
I feel like my old self again
Not there-there,
Here, here is the light!

14. Walk

Walk signifies a lot
You need not jog
If you wish for an erect spine
Walk!
Your walk signifies a lot
About you
To all who do not walk
Who you are...
What do you think
How's everything
Around you and within?
Why you are who you are?
How are you with others?
How do you make them feel about them?
What do you consider yourself...
A winner or a loser
A sinner or a saint
What time is it, lad
Your walk shall tell
Which phase are you undergoing
If not walking every day...
Walk along or walk alone
It's up to you
But walk in a way
Amid chaos

Night and day

That bewilderment leaves the palace

Confidence and inspiration reign every day

Walk even if a little for today

Your walk signifies a lot

About who you are, why you are as you are,

How you are if you are and most importantly what makes you

Whoever you are, odd or even

Nothing but your walk is enough to inform!

So, a session of walk a day

Keeps you healthy and fit

And makes you play long and befitting innings

Securing your security more than anything

Rest assured you are here to stay...

Not long before this day

These thoughts came to me

Walking all the way...

15. The Magic Within...

There is magic within
That a few do understand
We do carry within us
An eternal lamp
We chase elsewhere
When everything is to be found near
Why be a musk deer?
We need to contemplate and bare
We realise late
That we do carry useless weight
We need to give up on all uselessness
If we have to make any signs of progress
It is up to us
How we give in to the process
And don't hope, but make
Things that can do wonders for us
Is now only a moment's wait
A magic that we have been searching
Now for years
Is knocking at our gates...

16. Things like these

Stars shine bright in the night sky
Although, they have always been up there in the skies
Similarly in life
When darkness engulfs us all from all sides...
Left, right, front and behind...
We shine the brightest with our core strength
Even goats find their inner potential
To stand on two's
And fill themselves with energy
And they climb...
In life, if required, they jump as if there is no tomorrow...
Awaiting them anytime!

17. Heroism

Heroes are not born
They grow from strength to strength
With all they have got
Heroes don't have unusual horns
They can fly without flights
Yes indeed, they can soar high
Heroes don't manipulate
They take it on the chin,
No bad blood, no hate
Heroes are divine
In one life
They live millions of lives
No tide is high
Enough to knock them down
Heroes don't frown
They find the surplus even in the minus
Heroes do count
The blessings in disguise
Unlike modern man who always shouts!

18. God in Solitude

Why is there so much misery in this world?
Why did God create multiple?
Why doesn't he trample everything under His foot?
What is the wait for?
All the smiles on his face
Won't fade into mere oblivion
It took Him time to gather them
He enjoys the company of His creations
More than anything else
Eluded, we cannot be
He is a forever witness to everything
Earlier He was alone
The problem arose,
When he started feeling
Lonely, to the core
I cannot say about the rest
But this world in which I find myself
contributing something if not more is asleep
This world does not realize that
Dukkha begets more Dukkha
Pain is the Source
The origin of all creations: Sorrow
How could we expect this world to be
a great place to live in for tomorrow?
The Primordial Being

Felt lonely
It pained him to feel like a loner
The child in Him
Resisted His conscience
In the decision-making process
And here we are a product of that Store
The storehouse of optimism
Forgot about everything else
While creating something new
He forgot about his pain, his sorrow, his misery
Similarly, we too cannot afford
To brood and lament, and curse our destinies

19. Signs of God

In every act of yours find God's signs
Rummage through your life but find...
Kill small talk
And every work that you take up
In your life
Will be fine
God throws forward
Ideas
Perhaps not as sleek
As you would have expected
Going forward in life
In front of you are Ideas;
IDEAS that raise their heads and create
IDENTITIES in your mind...
You manifest
You attract
The things
That God wills
You create
You lose ideas
You die a pauper
Every tinge of fury
Inside
Let it burn out
For Mankind

In your head

Should be one voice

Fortitude, my God...

Fortitude my Lord,

Fortitude...

My God is pleased with me...

My Lord defines infinite joy for me...

My God is just, my God is fine,

my LORD is that well infinite...

20. Unconditional Strength Within

Everything is easy when you believe in yourself

Everything seems tough when you have to depend on others for help

You suffer, often unbearable, till you depend...

There's a sense of pain... a feeling of loss...as if you were losing yourself...

and you don't know...

There's no cure to it till you liberate the self

Create your help, and liberate yourself

Prosper in ways more than prosperity teaches

Despite being unconventional

People can triumph

In various ways...

Till you do, you have to keep your temper and self-confidence

At their respective places

Don't ask for it, go, win it, yourself...

Even if it is wayward in the initial stage

Gradually everything will fall into place

Mark my words, wordsmith

You ought to triumph in the end...

21. Hallowed Name

With every breadth
Take God's name
God is merciful
He'll show you the way
Pain and joy are like
Alternate days
They are sooner than later
Passing Away...
Whether you realise it or not
What's in a name...
Take God's name
That is the way
We all are not here
Forever to stay...
Stay with the name
Continue your part in the game
Duality creates anxiety
Non-duality relieves us
From all pains...
What's in a name?
That's the game...
Just keep playing;
you stay...
All sorts of alien presence
Will vanish into thin air

Conditions will favour
Inalienability again...
Inalienable is nothing
Work now for God's grace!

22. Ruminate

With you as my charioteer
I have nothing to fear
Your worthy name has come out of my mouth!
How won't I attain thee, that goes without saying...
I hold your hallowed feet within this heart
I take your holy name
I've received your grains
As Maa Annapurna, thou hast greatly blessed me time and again
With thy blessings upon me as Lord Shiva in Kaashi, I feel like Nandi
- the Bull devotee
Your blessings in the form of a garland garlanded around my neck like
Vasuki
Decked up with the ornament of your name
I sing thy glory
I sing thy praise
You followed me or I found you wherever I went...
I don't know whether you serve me or I serve thee
I know nothing about anything
Except for your hallowed omnipresence, I feel...
I don't know whether you look after me and my welfare from time to
time
or that I do, unknowingly...

23. Forsaken

Flung up

As high as the heavens

Thrown down

To the nether planes

Dig earth

Dig towns

Nowhere would you find

A second of this kind

Had it not been His will to create

Another Lord Rama - The Divine

Forsaken by the society

They lived holy

Gods for a reason truly

Sacrifices both big and small

Takes a lot out of us all

Nowhere would you see sacrifices of these scales

How under the Sun did they manage to make peace

With whatever they received as their destiny prevails?

One Rama killed his mother on his father's command and thereafter requested

her life back along with those of his brothers whom he had killed earlier

And another Rama pushed aside the thoughts of the crown and went happily to live in the wild

with his wife and step-brother to serve his father's command, who had promises to be kept to his wife, Rama's stepmother...

On an exile with a smile

Wow! Simply, how?

Both never questioned their father's good faith...

Some magic is in this name, Rama

How can they enjoy

What we cannot

Even though sacrifices

Of their stature were never made

On our part while living on this earth

They are Gods

Immortal for their deeds

No, looking back, till we achieve

A taste of the Godhood we do need...

24. Longing Ongoing...

Longing ongoing long enough
for the length of lifetimes...
For anyone to forbear
Any number of transmigrations
Your unswerving grace becomes Indispensable O Supreme, One with
All,
Things Divine
I was fed to my fill
For all these years
In all lifetimes
I wonder how these years
Kept changing in front of twin eyes...
O Heavenly Being with you as my only constant...
Companion for lifetimes...
Hand-holding me at all times...
I came this far...
Just impossible became possible
All because of you on my side
You never left me wailing aside
You are The One who accepted me
In my skin
O how grateful I am to thy honour
O Divine...
Is anything but you
Good Enough?

I ask thee
O wish-fulfilling tree
I have taken refuge in thou
The Supreme Banyan
You are the foremost authority
Brahman or Consciousness in me
Kindly be fruitful to each and all...
This is what I ask for...
Won't you help me?

25. Hallowed Presence

Knock-knock!

Who's there?

Not there, I'm here

At the door of your heart

I'm the porter of all your lives

And I don't carry the baggage of your past

Can I ask you?

The want of what...

brings you here?

Why did you even leave me to suffer at the hands of players?

Now, who is looking after me and my needs?

I have to do it all by myself; just telling...

Just dropping in a surprise visit

To wish "take care"

Won't do anything!

It won't be of much good use, seriously

No seriously, it can never be enough

At least for me, that is what I feel

And in my case

Is it even worthwhile to face the challenges that test the very core of

my being...

You're taking me wrong after all these years past...

Glad! We met at last!

Don't take me wrong, I have not wronged you, no-never-ever!

I have been here since time immemorial, knocking continuously ever
since without fail...
Only you were oblivious to the voice of your heart...
Finally, it's time, and you've heard!
Without much ado, I tell thee
The mortifying ordeals, the trials, and tribulations of life are of my will
As I know, success is counted sweetest
When earned through challenges, hurts, and difficulties...
I appreciate the things done!
You have had the guts to put in all the required efforts
To endure all aches; heroics like a stoic's son
A lot of hard work and perseverance, you've shown,
Of late
Being a person of substance affords you
The leverage to get things done
Without wait
Everything is Worthwhile!
Everything is worth the wait!
I know that!
All I can say is think about your heart...
Speak your heart...
It's a game of thought processes,
collocations weave a fine thread, and nothing else...

26. Sumptuous Meal

I had a sumptuous meal
Still, it feels as if incomplete
Of experiences, bitter and sweet
I have been served on my platter
Both these things
I'm reminiscing...

27. Voice of God

You, the almighty,
Be the voice I speak and sing...
Make me placid, sweet and docile,
I pray to thee...
Turn your infinite grace upon grace
And make me ever-free
I listen to your eternal voice O God
It is always heard within me
When the mind is indrawn
Withdrawn, and other-worldly
And the heart wants a joyride
With the joyrider who paces gleefully
I cherish your presence inside me...
Forever indebted to thee...
Forever indebted to thee...
Lo! There goes your majestic voice unworldly!

28. Dispassion

The distaste for worldly-wise
Has crept into your heart
Congratulations
You have come this far
With your perseverance
You've shown
Worldliness doesn't attract you
You don't get bothered
To the core
You are other-wise
You are other-worldly
Who is not to fall into the mire of worldliness…
And visit the nether world in no time
This is indeed a blessing in disguise
That you are unlike others of your times
You've had to undergo a lot of hardships
To come this far after a good number of lives
Don't treat yourself as weak
You are endowed with strength from the divine
Don't regress after such great progress...
People long to jump out and you think of entering again
It's a trap...
And no, it's not fine
To commit similar mistakes again and again...
Over the course of time

29. God is a puzzle!

God is a puzzle,

A mystery

Which, we have to solve

On our own terms!

Uncertainty is the key here...

From your uncertainty

You'll move toward certainty

That's for sure

We all will, sooner or later...

Conditions applied, of course...

At birth, death, and rebirth!

Attain God, and all thoughts that cloud you will vanish into thin air!

30. Me and God

Going back home

I will evaporate as smoke

No discomforts, no pains

Only me and God

Contemplate, and that's fine

No interpretations

No boundary lines

I dreamt an unusual dream

I don't know whether it has symbolism in it...

I dreamt, I ran across meadows,

a herd of elephants behind me,

I came across the wild, only to find a Royal Bengal tiger emerging,

ready to charge with a roar;

I ran behind to save my life,

I encountered a few deer, and

I ran for my life...

That is how my dream broke

And I found myself in the lap of God

Still, I consider

My story does not end here...